Uden Unicorn

Check out these other
Uden Unicorn
books!
Uden Unicorn Bottles, Boxes, and Bags
Uden Unicorn and the Royal Butterfly

Coming soon!
Uden Unicorn and the Runaway Rollercoaster

Writer and Illustrator: Jason Wilburn
Editor and Activities Writer: Tamara Wilburn
Photo and Illustration Contributor: Tucker Wilburn

First American Edition 2023
Second American Edition 2024
Copyright (C) 2024 Jason Wilburn
All rights reserved, including the right to reproduction in whole or in part in any form.

www.udenunicorn.com
ISBN: 9798336452631

Uden Unicorn's Playdate

With thanks
to efuture for opening the door,
Casey for the know-how,
and Patrick for the inspiration.

Uden likes making model knights.

"This knight has many parts," says Uden.

"I have more than ten knights in my collection."

Uden has collected knights for a long time.

"This is my first knight. I got it when I was three years old," Uden says.

"This knight does not have many parts. It's for little kids."

"Uden," calls Mom, "Mrs. Dragon is coming for a visit today."

Mrs. Dragon is very nice. But Uden doesn't care that she's visiting. She's Mom's friend.

"She will bring Dennis with her," Mom adds.

Now Uden is interested. Dennis is Mrs. Dragon's baby.

Uden loves babies. They're so cute. They always have such chubby cheeks.

"I've never met Dennis," says Uden. "Is he a little baby?"

"He's eighteen months old," says Mom.

"Oh..." thinks Uden. "So, he's one and a half."

"Do you have any toys that Dennis can play with," asks Mom. She opens Uden's closet.

"I just finished this model knight," says Uden.

"Oh no," says Mom. "That won't work. There are too many little pieces."

"That's what makes it so cool," says Uden.

"Dennis could swallow these little pieces," says Mom.

"Why would anyone swallow toys?" Uden thinks to himself.

Uden loves knights. And he wants Dennis to love knights too.

"What about this knight?" Uden asks.

"I've had it since I was a baby."

Mom looks at the knight. There are no small parts.

"I guess this will be OK," she says. "Are you sure?"

"Yes," says Uden. "And I can play with this one."

Uden takes out his second oldest knight.

Uden is excited when Mrs. Dragon arrives.

"Hi Una," she says to Mom. "Hi Uden."

"Hello Donna," says Mom. "Come on in."

Uden stares at Mrs. Dragon. She's very big.

"Where is Dennis?" asks Uden.

"Oh!" says Mrs. Dragon. "He's right here."

Mrs. Dragon steps to the side. Dennis is hiding behind her.

"Don't be shy," Mrs. Dragon tells Dennis. "This is Uden Unicorn."

Dennis Dragon looks at Uden.

"Uden wants to play with you," says Mom.

"We can play knights," says Uden.

Uden holds out one of the knights. Dennis comes closer and takes the toy.

"Doll," says Dennis.

Uden is surprised.

"It's not a doll!" he thinks. "I don't play with dolls!"

"Not 'doll,'" says Mrs. Dragon. "'Knight.'"

"Ni," says Dennis. "Ni! Ni! Ni!"

"He's learning many new words," explains Mrs. Dragon. "But it takes time."

"That's OK," says Uden. "Calling it a 'ni' is much better than calling it a doll."

"You sit there," says Uden, "and I'll sit over here."

Dennis sits on the floor holding his knight. He watches Uden.

"My knight will come to visit yours," Uden explains.

Uden walks his knight over to Dennis. Dennis laughs.

"Hello, sir knight," Uden says, playing. "Have you seen any dragons?"

"Ni!" says Dennis. "Ekky-ekky-ekky-ekky!"

Then, Dennis slams his knight into the floor.

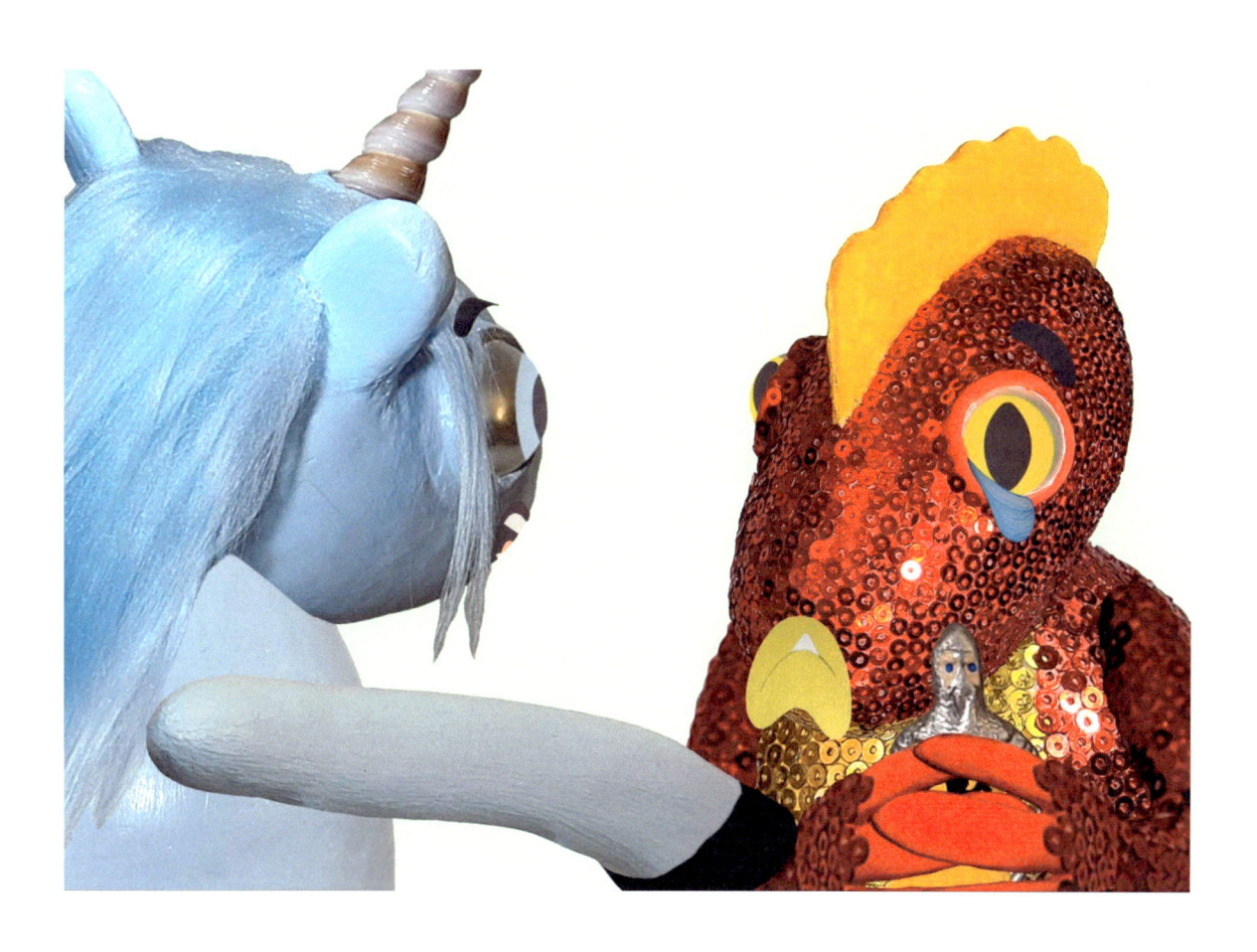

"No!" says Uden. "Be careful. You'll hurt him."

"Hurt?" asks Dennis. This is a word that Dennis knows.

Dennis's eyes start to fill with tears.

"It's OK," says Uden trying to calm Dennis down.

"Your game is a bit hard for Dennis," says Mom. "Try something else."

Uden thinks.

"Let's make our knights dance," says Uden.

Uden makes his knight jump and move. He sings a little song as his knight dances.

Dennis laughs loudly. He likes what Uden is doing.

Uden feels good. He likes that Dennis is laughing.

"Can you make your knight dance?" he asks Dennis.

Dennis opens his mouth. He puts Uden's knight in his mouth!

"AAAAAHHHHH!!!!" cries Uden in shock!

"What happened?" asks Mom.

"Dennis has my knight in his mouth!" cries Uden. Uden is not happy.

Mom and Mrs. Dragon look at each other. They are confused.

"Uden, that's how little kids play," explains Mom.

"Mmmmph-mmmm," says Dennis. Spit drips down the knight in his mouth.

"No!" cries Uden. He grabs the knight and pulls it from Dennis's mouth.

"Ni!" screams Dennis as he starts to cry.

"Uden!" shouts Mom in surprise.

But Uden has already run away. He locks himself in the bathroom.

Uden washes his knight in the sink.

"You look OK," Uden says to his knight. "You were almost eaten by a dragon!"

Then, Uden remembers. His other knight is still in the living room.

Uden peeks into the living room.

Dennis is no longer crying. He is playing with Uden's other knight.

"How can I save my knight before Dennis eats him?" wonders Uden.

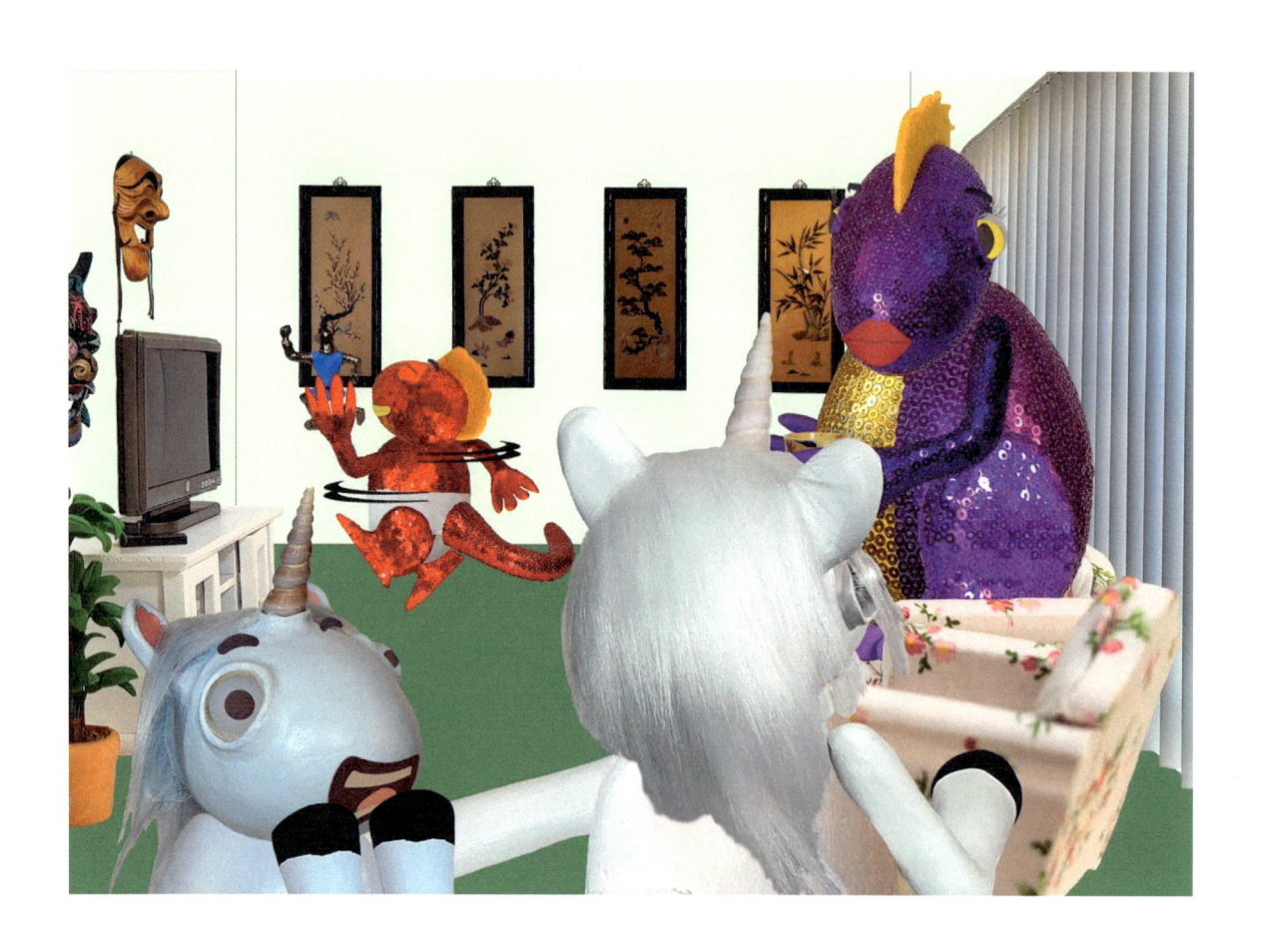

Uden tries to sneak into the living room. Mom sees him.

"Please excuse me for a moment, Donna," she says getting up.

Mom walks Uden into his room.

"I'm sorry," says Mom. "I guess you didn't understand how small kids play."

Uden is surprised. He thought Mom would yell at him.

"But," says Mom, "you shouldn't have pulled your toy away from Dennis."

"Dennis still has my other knight," says Uden. "I think he might hurt it."

"Well, let's find a better toy for Dennis to play with," says Mom.

Mom and Uden look in the closet.

"How about this ball?" asks Mom.

Mom and Uden go back to the living room. Uden has the ball.

"Ball!" says Dennis, happily. He drops the knight and looks at Uden.

"Dennis likes the ball more than my knight," says Uden.

"Yes, 'ball,'" says Uden. "Do you want to play?"

Dennis and Uden roll the ball back and forth. Uden doesn't worry about his ball getting hurt.

...even when Dennis puts it in his mouth.

Uden lets Dennis keep the ball.

"Goodbye, Dennis," says Uden as they head out the door.

"Bye bye!" says Dennis.

"Dennis was different than I expected," says Uden. "Having a baby around is a lot of work."

"Yes," agrees Mom. "But it can be nice too."

Uden's Crazy Story

For each of the numbers below, write words of your choosing for each part of speech. Read your words when you see the matching numbers in the story. Some word forms will change slightly. (You'll see.)

You can make many different stories by changing the words again and again!

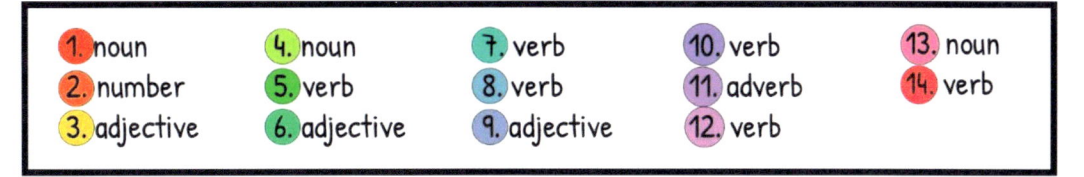

1. noun	4. noun	7. verb	10. verb	13. noun
2. number	5. verb	8. verb	11. adverb	14. verb
3. adjective	6. adjective	9. adjective	12. verb	

Uden Unicorn likes to collect (1). He has (2) of them in his collection. Uden wants to share his (3) (1) with Dennis.

Dennis is a (4). Are Uden's (1) right for Dennis? Mom (5) at Uden's (3) (1). She thinks it will be OK.

Mrs. Dragon is very (6). Uden (7) at her. But where is Dennis? Dennis is (8) behind his mom! Dennis is (9).

"Uden wants to (10) with you," Mrs. Dragon says.

Uden shows Dennis his (3) (1). Dennis smiles (11). The two friends sit on the floor. Uden makes his (1) (12). Dennis laughs.

"Can you make your (1) (12)?" asks Uden,

Dennis does not make his (1) (12). Instead, Dennis puts his (1) in his (13)! Uden (14).

Check out Uden Unicorn Readers for comprehension and vocabulary activities as well as more fun and games!

We're glad you enjoyed Uden Unicorn!

Please share Uden with others when you're done with this book. Consider gifting this book to a younger friend or leaving it in a free Little Library.

Share Uden with more people with the next few pages. Color your favorite page. Then, give your picture to a friend or hang it (with permission) on a community board.

Uden Unicorn
udenunicorn.com

Uden Unicorn

Uden Unicorn's Playdate

Uden Unicorn

Made in the USA
Columbia, SC
03 November 2024